Aussie Slang

Phrasebook Guide

Your Essential Guide to Navigating Australian Language and Culture

Introduction to Aussie Culture

Welcome to "Fair Dinkum Aussie Talk"—your go-to guide for navigating the quirky, colorful world of Australian slang! Whether you're planning your first trip Down Under, or just keen to sound like a true blue Aussie, this book is here to help you decode the lingo and blend in like a local.

Inside, you'll find themed chapters that cover everything from dining and drinking to navigating the outback, all packed with slang terms, pronunciations, definitions, and examples. Each entry is designed to be easy to understand and fun to use, with cultural insights sprinkled throughout to give you a taste of the Aussie lifestyle.

To get the most out of this book, flip to the section that suits your current situation—whether you're ordering a flat white, making new mates, or just trying to understand what the heck someone means by "fair dinkum." Use the examples and tips to practice and soon enough, you'll be chatting away like you've lived in Australia your whole life.

So dive in, have a laugh, and get ready to embrace the Aussie way of speaking—because here in Australia, it's all about keeping it light, fun, and a little bit cheeky!

Chapter 1:

Essential Aussie Slang for Travelers

G'day

Pronunciation:

guh-DAY

The core concept of:

A common greeting in Australia, equivalent to "hello" or "hi.

Real-world implementation:

"G'day, mate! How's it going?"
"G'day! Welcome to Australia!"

Arvo

Pronunciation:

AH-voh

The core concept of:

Short for "afternoon."

Real-world implementation:

"This Arvo is perfect for a coffee."
"It's been a hot arvo, hasn't it?"

Bogan

Pronunciation:

BOH-gun

The core concept of:

A derogatory term for someone perceived as unsophisticated or uncultured, often used humorously

Real-world implementation:

- "He's a bit of a bogan, but he's got a heart of gold."
- "That's such a bogan thing to do!"

Brekkie

Pronunciation:

BREK-ee

The core concept of:

Short for "breakfast."

Real-world implementation:

- "Let's go grab some brekkie at the café."
- "What did you have for brekkie this morning?"

Thongs

Pronunciation:

THONGS

The core concept of:

Flip-flops or sandals. In Australia, "thongs" refers to footwear, not underwear.

Real–world implementation:

- "Don't forget your thongs when we hit the beach!"
- "I wear thongs all summer long."

Servo

Pronunciation:

SER-voh

The core concept of:

Short for "service station" or "gas station."

Real-world implementation:

- "Let's stop at the servo to fill up the tank."
- "I'll grab a drink from the servo."

Macca's

Pronunciation:

MAK-uhz

The core concept of:

The Australian nickname for McDonald's

Real-world implementation:

- "Fancy a bite at Macca's?"
- "We stopped at Macca's for lunch on the road trip."

No Worries

Pronunciation:

noh WUR-eez

The core concept of:

A phrase used to say "It's okay," "Don't worry about it," or "You're welcome."

Real-world implementation:

- "Thanks for helping out."
- "No worries, mate!"
- "No worries, it's all good!"

Fair Dinkum

Pronunciation:

Fair DIN-kum

The core concept of:

Genuine, real, or true. Can be used to express disbelief or confirm something's authenticity.

Real-world implementation:

- "Is that fair dinkum?" (Is that true?)
- "He's a fair dinkum Aussie."

Ta

Pronunciation:

tah

The core concept of:

A casual way of saying "thank you."

Real-world implementation:

- "Ta for the lift!"
- "Here's your coffee."
- "Ta!"

Chapter 2:

Navigating the Cities and Outback

Bush

Pronunciation:

boo-SH

The core concept of:

Refers to rural, undeveloped land in Australia, often dense with vegetation, but can also mean the outback or countryside in general.

Real—world implementation:

- "We're heading out to the bush for the weekend."
- "He's a real bushman, knows his way around the wild."

Outback

Pronunciation:

OUT-back

The core concept of:

The remote, sparsely populated interior regions of Australia, known for its harsh environment.

Real-world implementation:

- "You'll need plenty of water if you're driving through the outback."
- "The outback is where you'll find true Aussie wilderness."

CBD (Central Business District)

Pronunciation:

SEE-BEE-DEE

The core concept of:

The main commercial and business area of a city, often in the city center.

Real-world implementation:

- "We're staying in a hotel right in the CBD."
- "The CBD is where you'll find all the big shops and offices."

Ute

Pronunciation:
YOOT

The core concept of:
A utility vehicle, often a pickup truck, commonly used in both urban and rural areas of Australia.

Real-world implementation:
- "We loaded the gear into the back of the ute."
- "Utes are perfect for carrying tools and equipment in the outback."

Ripper

Pronunciation:

RIP-uh

The core concept of:

Excellent, fantastic, or really good; often used to describe a great event, experience or thing.

Real-world implementation:

- "That sunset over the outback was a ripper!"
- "We had a ripper time exploring the city."

Bottle-O

Pronunciation:

BOT-ul-oh

The core concept of:

A liquor store or bottle shop.

Real-world implementation:

- "Let's stop at the Bottle-O to grab some drinks before heading out."
- "Every small town has a Bottle-O somewhere."

Roadie

Pronunciation:

ROH-dee

The core concept of:

A drink taken "on the road," usually referring to an alcoholic beverage consumed while traveling (though not while driving).

Real-world implementation:

- "Grab a roadie for the drive back to the city."
- "We picked up some roadies at the Bottle-O before leaving town."

Trackie Dacks

Pronunciation:

TRAK-ee DAKS

The core concept of:

Slang for tracksuit pants, often worn for comfort, particularly when traveling long distances.

Real-world implementation:

- "I'm just going to wear my trackie dacks for the road trip."
- "Trackie dacks are perfect for a comfy drive."

Swag

Pronunciation:

SWAG

The core concept of:

A portable sleeping unit, typically used for camping in the outback. It's a bedroll with bedding inside, often waterproof.

Real-world implementation:

- "We set up our swags under the stars."
- "A swag is all you need for a night in the bush."

Cuppa

Pronunciation:

CUP-ah

The core concept of:

A cup of tea or coffee; often a comforting drink after a long day of travel.

Real-world implementation:

- "After that long drive, I could really go for a cuppa."
- "Nothing beats a cuppa in the morning before heading out."

Chapter 3:

Dining and Drinking in Australia

Barbie

Pronunciation:

BAR-bee

The core concept of:

Short for "barbecue," a popular social gathering where food is cooked on a grill, typically outdoors.

Real-world implementation:

- "We're having a barbie this weekend —bring your own meat!"
- "Nothing beats a barbie on a sunny arvo."

Snags

Pronunciation:

SNAGS

The core concept of:

Sausages, often cooked on a barbecue.

Real-world implementation:

- "Throw some snags on the barbie, will ya?"
- "I'll grab a couple of snags from the butcher for dinner."

Chook

Pronunciation:

CHOOK

The core concept of:

Slang for chicken, often used to refer to a roast or cooked chicken.

Real-world implementation:

- "We're having roast chook for dinner."
- "Pick up a chook from the shop on your way home."

Sanger

Pronunciation:

SANG-uh

The core concept of:

A sandwich

Real–world implementation:

- "I'm packing a sanger for lunch."
- "You can't go wrong with a good ham and cheese sanger."

Brekkie

Pronunciation:

BREK-ee

The core concept of:

Short for "breakfast."

Real-world implementation:

- "Let's grab some brekkie before we hit the road."
- "Aussies love their big brekkies on the weekends."

Tinnie

Pronunciation:

TIN-ee

The core concept of:

A can of beer

Real–world implementation:

- "Crack open a tinnie, mate!"
- "We brought a few tinnies for the beach."

Esky

Pronunciation:

ES-kee

The core concept of:

A portable cooler used to keep drinks and food cold, especially during outdoor activities.

Real-world implementation:

- "Don't forget the esky for the barbie."
- "We packed the esky with drinks and snacks for the picnic."

Flat White

Pronunciation:

flat WHY-t

The core concept of:

A popular Australian coffee made with espresso and steamed milk, similar to a latte but with less foam.

Real-world implementation:

- "I'll have a flat white, please."
- "Flat whites are the go-to coffee for many Aussies."

Bikkie

Pronunciation:

BIK-ee

The core concept of:

A biscuit or cookie.

Real-world implementation:

- "Would you like a cuppa and a bikkie?"
- "I always have a bikkie with my afternoon tea."

Pub Grub

Pronunciation:

PUB grub

The core concept of:

Food served in a pub, often hearty and filling dishes like steak, pies, and burgers

Real-world implementation:

- "Let's grab some pub grub for dinner tonight."
- "You can't beat pub grub after a long day."

Chapter 4:

Aussie Sports and Recreation

Footy

Pronunciation:

FOOT-ee

The core concept of:

Short for Australian Rules Football (AFL), a popular sport in Australia, though it can also refer to rugby in some regions.

Real-world implementation:

- "We're heading to the oval to watch some footy this arvo."
- "He's mad about footy, never misses a game."

Cricket

Pronunciation:

CRIK-it

The core concept of:

A bat-and-ball game popular in Australia, often played in parks and backyards.

Real-world implementation:

- "We're having a game of cricket in the park this weekend."
- "The Aussies are dominating in cricket this season."

Nippers

Pronunciation:

NIP-uhz

The core concept of:

A junior program run by surf lifesaving clubs for young children to learn about surf safety and lifesaving skills.

Real-world implementation:

- "The kids are joining Nippers this summer."
- "Nippers is great for teaching beach safety early on."

Thongs

Pronunciation:

THONGS

The core concept of:

Flip-flops or sandals. Common footwear in Australia, especially at the beach or during casual outdoor activities.

Real-world implementation:

- "Don't forget your thongs when we head to the beach."
- "Thongs are all you need for a day in the sun."

Walkabout

Pronunciation:

WALK-uh-bout

The core concept of:

A term traditionally used to describe a journey taken by Indigenous Australians, but also used informally to mean going for a walk or wandering.

Real-world implementation:

- "I'm going on a walkabout through the bush this weekend."
- "He's been on a bit of a walkabout lately, exploring the outback."

Mate

Pronunciation:

MAYT

The core concept of:

A friendly term for a friend or companion, commonly used in social and sporting contexts.

Real-world implementation:

"Good on ya, mate! That was a great goal!"
- "Thanks for helping out, mate."

Surf's Up

Pronunciation:

SURF-zup

The core concept of:

A phrase used to indicate that the waves are good for surfing, or to express excitement about surfing

Real-world implementation:

- "Surf's up, let's hit the waves!"
- "He's always excited when surf's up."

Sausage Sizzle

Pronunciation:

SAW-sij SIZ-ul

The core concept of:

A popular Australian community fundraising event where sausages are cooked on a barbecue and sold to raise money.

Real-world implementation:

- "Grab a snag at the sausage sizzle after the game."
- "There's a sausage sizzle at the local footy match this weekend."

Ripper

Pronunciation:

RIP-uh

The core concept of:

Used to describe something that is excellent or fantastic, often in the context of a great play or an exciting moment in sports.

Real–world implementation:

- "That was a ripper of a goal!"
- "He had a ripper game, didn't miss a beat!"

Chapter 5:

Understanding Aussie Humor

Larrikin

Pronunciation:

LAR-ik-in

The core concept of:

A person who is cheeky, mischievous, and often playful in a good-natured way; someone with a good sense of humor.

Real-world implementation:

- "He's such a larrikin, always pulling pranks on his mates."
- "A true larrikin at heart, she had everyone laughing all night."

Taking the Piss

Pronunciation:

TAY-king the PISS

The core concept of:

To mock, tease, or joke around with someone in a light-hearted manner

Real-world implementation:

- "Don't get upset, mate, he's just taking the piss."
- "We're always taking the piss out of each other at work."

Fair Dinkum

Pronunciation:

FAIR DIN-kum

The core concept of:

Genuine, true, or honest; often used to express surprise or to confirm that something is real.

Real-world implementation:

- "Fair dinkum, that was the funniest thing I've ever seen!"
- "He's a fair dinkum bloke, always tells it like it is."

Deadset

Pronunciation:

DEAD-set

The core concept of:

Absolutely true or serious; often used to emphasize the truth or seriousness of something, including jokes.

Real-world implementation:

- "Deadset, that was the best prank ever!"
- "He's deadset hilarious, can't stop laughing when he's around."

Tall Poppy Syndrome

Pronunciation:

TALL POP-ee SIN-drome

The core concept of:

A cultural tendency to criticize or bring down people who are successful or who stand out, often done humorously in Australia.

Real-world implementation:

- "He's doing great, but watch out for tall poppy syndrome."
- "A bit of tall poppy syndrome there, just keeping things in check!"

Bloody

Pronunciation:

BLUD-ee

The core concept of:

A versatile intensifier used to express emphasis, often in humor or frustration.

Real–world implementation:

- "That was bloody hilarious!"
- "He's a bloody good comedian, isn't he?"

Ripper

Pronunciation:

RIP-uh

The core concept of:

Used to describe something that is excellent or fantastic, often in a humorous context.

Real-world implementation:

- "That was a ripper of a joke!"
- "He told a ripper story at the pub last night."

Dag

ronunciation:

AG

he core concept of:

n affectionate term for someone who is a
it uncool or quirky but in an endearing
nd often humorous way.

eal-world implementation:

- "You're such a dag, but we love you
  for it."
- "He's a bit of a dag, but he's got a
  great sense of humor."

Sledge

Pronunciation:

SLEDGE

The core concept of:

A form of verbal banter or trash talk, often used in sports to unsettle an opponent, but also used humorously among friends.

Real-world implementation:

- "He's the king of sledging on the cricket field."
- "We were sledging each other all day, it was a laugh."

Chockers

Pronunciation:

CHOK-uhz

The core concept of:

Completely full or packed, often used in a humorous way to describe how crowded or busy something is.

Real–world implementation:

- "The pub was chockers last night, couldn't move!"
- "It's chockers in here, where'd all these people come from?"

Chapter 6:

Shopping and Bargaining

Docket

Pronunciation:

DOCK-it

The core concept of:

A receipt or a proof of purchase, often used when shopping in Australia.

Real-world implementation:

- "Make sure you keep the docket in case you need to return it."
- "The cashier handed me the docket after I paid."

Heaps

Pronunciation:

HEEPS

The core concept of:

A term used to describe a large amount or quantity of something, often used when talking about shopping deals or quantities.

Real-world implementation:

- "They've got heaps of discounts at the sale."
- "I bought heaps of stuff at the market today."

Bottle-O

Pronunciation:
BOT-ul-oh

The core concept of:
A liquor store where you can buy alcoholic beverages; common in Australia.

Real-world implementation:
"I'm heading to the Bottle-O to grab some drinks."
"They've got a special at the Bottle-O today."

Spruiker

Pronunciation:

SPROO-ker

The core concept of:

A person who stands outside a store or market stall, loudly promoting goods to attract customers.

Real—world implementation:

- "The spruiker outside the shop was really convincing."
- "You can hear the spruikers all over the market on weekends."

Haggling

Pronunciation:

HAG-ling

The core concept of:

The process of negotiating a price, commonly done in markets or second-hand shops.

Real–world implementation:

- "I managed to haggle the price down at the market."
- "Don't be afraid to haggle when you're shopping here."

Bargain

Pronunciation:

BAR-gun

The core concept of:

A good deal or something bought at a low price; often used to describe successful haggling or finding discounted items.

Real-world implementation:

- "I found an absolute bargain at the second-hand shop."
- "These shoes were a real bargain, couldn't resist!"

Op Shop

Pronunciation:

OP shop

The core concept of:

Short for "opportunity shop," a thrift store where second-hand goods are sold, often run by charities.

Real—world implementation:

- "I found some great vintage clothes at the op shop."
- "Op shops are perfect for bargain hunting."

Mates Rates

Pronunciation:

MAYTS RAYTS

The core concept of:

A discounted price offered to friends or regular customers, a common practice in Australia.

Real-world implementation:

- "He gave me mates rates on the surfboard, saved a heap!"
- "Ask for mates rates, you never know what you'll get."

Cark It

Pronunciation:

KARK it

The core concept of:

To break down or stop working, often used to describe second-hand items that might not last long.

Real-world implementation:

- "This old washing machine could cark it any day, but it's cheap."
- "I hope the car doesn't cark it before I get home."

Chuck In

Pronunciation:

CHUK in

The core concept of:

To include something extra for free, often used when negotiating or buying multiple items.

Real-world implementation:

- "If you buy this, I'll chuck in a free hat
- "They chucked in some extra goodies with my purchase."

Chapter 7:

Safety and Emergency Situations

Ambo

Pronunciation:

AM-bo

The core concept of:

An ambulance officer or paramedic; someone who responds to medical emergencies

Real–world implementation:

- "Call an ambo, he's hurt pretty bad!"
- "The ambo arrived just in time to help."

Triple Zero (000)

Pronunciation:

TRIP-ul ZEE-ro

The core concept of:

Australia's emergency number, equivalent to 911 in the United States; used for fire, police, or medical emergencies.

Real–world implementation:

- "If there's an emergency, just dial triple zero."
- "We had to call triple zero when the fire started."

Firie

Pronunciation:

FIY-ree

The core concept of:

A firefighter; someone who responds to fires and related emergencies

Real-world implementation:

- "The firies did a great job putting out the blaze."
- "If there's a fire, the firies will be on their way."

Cop

Pronunciation:

COP

The core concept of:

A police officer; someone who enforces the law and responds to crime and safety issues.

Real-world implementation:

"The cops are patrolling the area after the break-in."

"If you see anything suspicious, let the cops know."

Bushfire

Pronunciation:

BUSH-fyre

The core concept of:

A fire that burns in grasslands, forests, or the bush, common in Australia, especially during dry seasons.

Real-world implementation:

- "There's a bushfire warning in the area, stay alert."
- "The bushfire spread quickly due to the strong winds."

Rip

Pronunciation:

RIP

The core concept of:

A strong current that can pull swimmers out to sea; common in Australian beaches, requiring caution.

Real-world implementation:

- "Watch out for rips when swimming at the beach."
- "He got caught in a rip, but the lifeguards saved him."

Snakebite Kit

Pronunciation:

SNAKE-byt kit

The core concept of:

A first aid kit specifically designed to treat snake bites, essential for hiking or walking in the bush.

Real–world implementation:

- "Always carry a snakebite kit when you're out bushwalking."
- "He used the snakebite kit after spotting a brown snake."

SES (State Emergency Service)

Pronunciation:

ESS EE ESS

The core concept of:

A volunteer emergency organization that assists during floods, storms, and other natural disasters.

Real-world implementation:

- "The SES is helping with the flood evacuations."
- "Call the SES if you need assistance during the storm."

Surf Lifesaver

Pronunciation:

SURF LYF-say-vuh

The core concept of:

A person trained to rescue swimmers and ensure safety at the beach; often volunteers.

Real-world implementation:

- "The surf lifesaver warned us about strong currents."
- "Always swim near the surf lifesavers for your safety."

Grog

Pronunciation:

GROG

The core concept of:

Alcohol, often referring to beer or spirits; in the context of safety, it's important to be aware of grog-related risks.

Real-world implementation:

"He had too much grog and needed to be taken home."

"Be careful with grog, especially when swimming or driving."

Chapter 9:

Making Friends and Social Etiquette

Mate

Pronunciation:

MATE

The core concept of:

A common term for a friend or companion; used to address someone in a friendly manner.

Real-world implementation:

- "G'day, mate! How's it going?"
- "He's a good mate of mine, we've known each other for years."

Bloke

Pronunciation:

BLOKE

The core concept of:

Informal term for a man; similar to "guy" or "dude" in other English-speaking countries.

Real-world implementation:

- "He's a top bloke, always ready to help out."
- "I met this bloke at the game last night."

Sheila

Pronunciation:

SHEE-LAH

The core concept of:

Informal term for a woman; similar to "girl" or "lady" in other contexts.

Real-world implementation:

- "She's a great sheila, really knows how to have fun."
- "I met a sheila who's new in town."

Fair Go

Pronunciation:

FAIR GO

The core concept of:

A phrase meaning to give someone a chance or treat them fairly; used in social situations to encourage fairness and inclusivity

Real-world implementation:

- "Give him a fair go, he's new here."
- "Everyone deserves a fair go, don't be too harsh."

Chuffed

Pronunciation:

HUFFED

The core concept of:

Feeling pleased or delighted; used to express satisfaction or happiness.

Real-world implementation:

"I'm chuffed that you could make it to the party!"

"She was chuffed with the surprise gift."

Dodgy

Pronunciation:

DOD-JEE

The core concept of:

Something or someone that seems unreliable, suspicious, or potentially problematic; can be used humorously or critically.

Real-world implementation:

- "That place looks a bit dodgy, maybe we should try somewhere else."
- "He's known for his dodgy behavior, s be careful."

Bogan

Pronunciation:

BOH-GAN

The core concept of:

A somewhat derogatory term for someone perceived as unsophisticated or lower-class, often used humorously among friends.

Real–world implementation:

- "He's a bit of a bogan with his taste in clothes, but he's a good guy."
- "We had a laugh about how bogan the party was."

Up for It

Pronunciation:

UP FOR IT

The core concept of:

Willing or enthusiastic about participating in an activity or event.

Real-world implementation:

- "Are you up for it this weekend? We're going hiking."
- "She's always up for it when we plan a night out."

Aussie Salute

Pronunciation:

OZ-EE SAH-LOOT

The core concept of:

Waving your hand to shoo away flies; a common and humorous gesture in Australia.

Real—world implementation:

- "You'll get plenty of opportunities for an Aussie salute in the summer."
- "He was giving the Aussie salute the whole time we were outside."

Knackered

Pronunciation:

NACK-ERD

The core concept of:

Extremely tired or exhausted; used to describe feeling very worn out.

Real-world implementation:

- "After the long hike, I was completely knackered."
- "She looked knackered after the marathon."

Chapter 10:

Regional Slang Differences

Queenslander

Pronunciation:

KWEENZ-LAND-ER

The core concept of:

A term used to refer to people from Queensland; can also describe something typical of Queensland

Real-world implementation:

- "That's a real Queenslander way to handle the heat."
- "He's a true Queenslander, born and raised."

Westie

Pronunciation:

WES-TEE

The core concept of:

Informal term for someone from Western Sydney or Western Australia; can be used affectionately or pejoratively depending on context.

Real–world implementation:

- "He's a bit of a Westie, but he's got a heart of gold."
- "We're heading out to meet some Westies for dinner."

Melburnian

Pronunciation:

MEL-BUR-NEE-AN

The core concept of:

A term used to refer to people from Melbourne, often used to describe local attitudes or customs.

Real-world implementation:

- "Only a true Melburnian would know the best laneway cafes."
- "She's a proud Melburnian with a deep love for the arts."

Sandgroper

Pronunciation:

SAND-GRO-PER

The core concept of:

A nickname for people from Western Australia, particularly those from Perth; it can also refer to someone with a strong connection to WA.

Real-world implementation:

- "He's a Sandgroper through and through, always talking about WA."
- "You'll find lots of Sandgropers at the local footy games."

Hobartian

Pronunciation:

HO-BART-EE-AN

The core concept of:

A term used to refer to people from Hobart, Tasmania; can describe local customs or traits.

Real-world implementation:

- "The Hobartians have a great appreciation for local produce."
- "As a Hobartian, she's always excited about the next food festival."

Avid

ronunciation:

H-VID

he core concept of:

the context of Australian slang,
articularly in Sydney, it can refer to
omeone who is enthusiastic or passionate
bout something, often used with a
egional twist.

eal-world implementation:

"He's an avid surfer, always chasing
the best waves in Bondi."
"She's known for being an avid fan of
local Sydney bands."

Digger

Pronunciation:

DIG-ER

The core concept of:

In some regions, especially in the context of Australian World War II history, it refers to an Australian soldier; more generally, it can also mean a hardworking person.

Real-world implementation:

- "My grandfather was a digger in the war."
- "He's a real digger, always working hard on the farm."

Knickers

Pronunciation:

NIK-ERS

The core concept of:

In some regions, particularly in Victoria, it refers to underwear or panties; it can also be used informally in a humorous or affectionate way.

Real-world implementation:

- "I need to buy new knickers before our trip."
- "She laughed when he said he'd lost his knickers."

Togs

Pronunciation:

TOGS

The core concept of:

A term used in Queensland and other regions to refer to swimwear or bathing suits

Real-world implementation:

- "Don't forget your togs for the beach tomorrow."
- "She bought new togs for the summer holidays."

Brolly

Pronunciation:

BROL-LEE

The core concept of:

A casual term for an umbrella, used in various parts of Australia

Real-world implementation:

- "Grab your brolly, it's going to rain later."
- "I left my brolly at home and got soaked."

Conclusion and Travel Tips

Final Advice for Travelers on How to Use Slang Effectively

Using Australian slang can greatly enhance your travel experience by helping you connect with locals and fully immerse yourself in the culture. Here are some final tips for using slang effectively:

Observe and Listen: Pay attention to how locals use slang in conversations. Listening and observing will help you understand the context and nuances of different terms. This will also give you a sense of when and how to use slang appropriately.

Start with Common Terms: Begin by learning and using commonly used slang terms, such as "mate" and "arvo." These are widely recognized and understood, and using them will help you sound more natural in conversations.

Use Slang Appropriately: Ensure that you use slang in the right context. Avoid using terms that you're not familiar with, as this might lead to misunderstandings or come across as inauthentic. It's best to use slang in informal settings and with people who are comfortable with casual language.

Ask for Clarification: If you hear a slang term that you don't understand, don't hesitate to ask for clarification. Australians are generally friendly and appreciate your interest in their language and culture. Asking questions shows that you're engaged and eager to learn.

5. Be Mindful of Regional Variations: Be aware that slang can vary significantly between regions in Australia. What might be common in Sydney may not be used or understood in Melbourne or Perth. Adjust your usage based on your location and the people you're interacting with.

6. Avoid Stereotyping: Use slang respectfully and avoid stereotypes. Slang is a part of cultural identity and should be used in a way that shows respect for its origins and meaning. Avoid using terms that could be considered derogatory or offensive.

7. Practice and Engage: The best way to become comfortable with slang is to practice using it in conversations. Engage with locals, participate in social activities, and don't be afraid to incorporate slang into your everyday language.

Additional Tips for a Smooth and Enjoyable Trip to Australia

Plan Ahead: Research your destinations and plan your itinerary in advance. Australia is a large country with diverse regions, so understanding the local attractions, climate, and travel options will help you make the most of your trip.

Stay Hydrated and Sun Safe: Australia's climate can be quite hot, especially in the summer. Make sure to drink plenty of water and use sunscreen to protect yourself from the sun. Wearing a hat and sunglasses can also help shield you from UV rays.

Embrace the Outdoors: Take advantage of Australia's stunning natural landscapes. Whether it's exploring the Great Barrier Reef, hiking in national parks, or relaxing on beautiful beaches, make outdoor activities a part of your trip.

Respect Wildlife and Nature: Australia is home to unique wildlife and natural environments. Follow local guidelines for interacting with animals and respect nature by sticking to designated paths and areas.

Use Public Transport: Australia's cities have efficient public transport systems. Consider using buses, trains, and ferries to get around, as they can be convenient and cost-effective ways to explore.

Learn About Local Customs: Familiarize yourself with Australian customs and etiquette. This includes tipping practices, dining manners, and social norms. Understanding these will help you navigate social interactions smoothly.

7. Carry Cash and Cards: While most places accept credit and debit cards, it's a good idea to carry som cash for smaller purchases or places that might not accept cards.

8. Stay Connected: Make sure you have access to a reliable mobile phone plan or Wi-Fi to stay connected. This will help you with navigation, communication, and accessing travel information.

9. Emergency Numbers: Be aware of emergency contact numbers in Australia. For any emergencies, dial 000 for police, fire, or medical assistance.

10. Enjoy the Experience: Australia offers a wide range of experiences, from vibrant city life to tranquil natural settings. Take the time to explore, enjoy local cuisine, and immerse yourself in the unique culture and lifestyle.

By following these tips and embracing Australian slang and culture, you'll be well-prepared for an enjoyable and memorable trip to Australia. Have a fantastic journey and make the most of your Australian adventure!

Printed in Great Britain
by Amazon

54292474R00059